THE BLACK SUNDAY DUST BLIZZARD

A DAY THAT CHANGED AMERICA

by Bruce Berglund

CAPSTONE PRESS
a capstone imprint

Published by Capstone Press, an imprint of Capstone
1710 Roe Crest Drive, North Mankato, Minnesota 56003
capstonepub.com

Library of Congress Cataloging-in-Publication Data is available on the Library of Congress website.
ISBN 9781666341508 (library binding)
ISBN 9781666341515 (paperback)
ISBN 9781666341522 (eBook PDF)

Summary: The 1930s were a tough time. The Great Depression left many people jobless and penniless. Dust storms and drought led to failed crops. People thought things couldn't get much worse. Then, on April 14, 1935, the sky turned black. For hours, an enormous dust blizzard blanketed the country in darkness. Step back in time to learn about what led up to this terrifying storm, how the tragic event unfolded, and the ways in which one dark day changed America forever.

Editorial Credits
Editor: Book Buddy Media

Consultant Credits
Richard Bell
Associate Professor, Department of History
University of Maryland
College Park, Maryland

Image Credits
Alamy: Everett Collection Historical, 6, Volgi archive, 7; Associated Press, 22; Getty Images: Bert Garai, 23, MCT, 17, Transcendental Graphics, 16; Library of Congress: Farm Security Administration - Office of War Information, Cover, U.S. Farm Security Administration/Office of War Information, 25; Shutterstock: D Guest Smith, 27, Everett Collection, 5, 10, 13, 15, 20, 21; The New York Public Library: Farm Security Administration Photographs/Arthur Rothstein, 12, Dorothea Lange, 11, Russell Lee, 14, National Highways Association: Photographs, 9; Wikimedia: Library of Congress/Lucullus V. McWhorter, 8, R.E. Briola, USDA Natural Resources Conservation Service, 26, US National Oceanic and Atmospheric Administration, 19

All internet sites appearing in back matter were available and accurate when this book was sent to press.

Source Notes
"It was terrible . . . " Scruggs, Marg. Oral History Interview. "The Dust Bowl: Dust, Drought, and Dreams Gone Dry." Judith J. Carrier Library. Tarrant County College Library, March 10, 2021. https://libguides.tccd.edu/c.php?g=240523&p=1623191, Accessed January 18, 2022.

"Dust to breathe . . . " Henderson, Caroline. "Letters from the Dust Bowl." The Atlantic, May 1936. https://www.theatlantic.com/magazine/archive/1936/05/letters-from-the-dust-bowl/308897/, Accessed January 18, 2022.

"We couldn't get in the house . . . " Brown, Trixie Travis. Documentary Interview. "Trixie Travis Brown Talks About Black Sunday." The Dust Bowl, PBS. November 18, 2012. https://www.pbs.org/video/dust-bowl-trixie-travis-brown-talks-about-black-sunday/, Accessed January 18, 2022.

"Residents of the southwestern dust bowl..." Geiger, Robert. Quoted in "The Black Sunday Dust Storm of April 14, 1935." National Weather Service. https://www.weather.gov/oun/events-19350414, Accessed January 18, 2022.

Printed and bound in the USA. 4882

TABLE OF CONTENTS

Words in **bold** are in the glossary.

April 14, 1935, started as a beautiful day on the Great Plains. For weeks, the wind had been blowing dust across the prairie in Texas, Oklahoma, Kansas, eastern Colorado, and northeastern New Mexico. But the sky was clear this morning. People went outside to enjoy the sunshine.

The weather changed quickly. The wind grew strong. It lifted soil from dry fields. People on the Great Plains had seen dust storms before. This, though, was something different. Even with windows closed, rooms filled with dust. Outside, it was black as night. People called the day Black Sunday.

When Black Sunday happened, the Great Plains was in the middle of a long **drought**. Crops died. Fields were empty. The area became known as the Dust Bowl.

Many people left the Dust Bowl. Farmers who stayed had to raise crops in different ways. They never wanted to go through a day like Black Sunday again. It was a day that changed the nation.

During the Dust Bowl, states between the Appalachian and Rocky Mountains experienced droughts and blowing dust.

CHAPTER 1

A HOME ON THE PLAINS

At the start of the 1900s, many people in the United States moved west into the Great Plains. Some wanted to leave cities to seek a new life. Others were **immigrants** who had come from Europe. A number were Black Americans who wanted to farm their own land.

Nicodemus, Kansas, was settled by Black homesteaders in the late 1800s.

In 1862, Congress had passed a law called the **Homestead** Act. This allowed people who moved to the plains to own the land where they settled. These people became known as homesteaders.

The Great Plains is a dry area. Not much rain falls. But homesteaders believed if they removed the prairie grass, the soil would hold water. They plowed up the dry prairie land and planted wheat, corn, and other crops.

Four million homestead claims were made across 30 different states.

During the 1920s, there was more rain than usual, so crops grew well. And farmers now had gas-powered tractors and harvesters. They could farm more land and bring in more crops. The opportunities seemed endless, just like the open prairie reaching to the horizon.

The Homestead Act forced Native Americans from their homes. Between 1887 and 1937, 65 percent of their land had been stolen.

THE HOMESTEAD ACT

The original Homestead Act allowed any citizen to claim 160 acres (64.7 hectares) of land in the Great Plains and western United States. If that person lived on the land for five years and built a house or a farm, then they became owner of the land. Between 1862 and 1934, the Homestead Act granted ownership for 1.6 million homesteads.

Farm tractors of the 1920s and 1930s did many jobs, including pulling road graders.

The lands claimed by homesteaders had been home to different Native American tribes. Native communities grew crops and hunted bison and other animals. But the U.S. government wanted homesteaders to take ownership of the land and use it for farms and ranches. The government believed that if individual people owned land, it would produce more. To make room for homesteaders, the government forced Native Americans onto reservations.

CHAPTER 2

DROUGHT ARRIVES

Farmers planted more crops in the 1920s. They grew wheat, corn, and cotton. Towns grew larger. Some places doubled their population during this decade.

Farmers worked together to harvest their crops.

But farmers were working the land too hard. The Great Plains had only a thin layer of topsoil. This is the layer of soil that plants grow in. When tractors plowed a new field, they churned up this topsoil. **Nutrients** in the topsoil fed the growing crops. But year after year, the nutrients were depleted.

The unusually high rainfall started to decline. Starting in 1931, rainfall on the Great Plains was far below normal. Crops dried out in the fields.

FACT
Today, farmers can dig deep wells to **irrigate** their fields. They also use chemical fertilizers to add nutrients to the soil. During the 1930s, neither of these were things farmers could do.

People did not have a way to artificially water their crops. Without rain, there was no water.

The Great Depression (1929–1939) began. The price of wheat and other crops fell. Because farmers were making less money, they tried to plant on even more land. They hoped that harvesting more would make up for the low prices.

More farmland meant more plains grass to dig up. The farmers planted their usual crops. But without rain, the crops died. There were not enough nutrients in the soil to help crops grow when there was rain. The soil dried out and turned to dust. Without plants growing, nothing held the dry soil in place.

Blowing dust created drifts 2 to 3 feet (0.6 to 0.9 meters) high—or even higher. Farmers raised fences so they wouldn't get buried in the drifting sand.

People in cities could not even try to grow their own food. They waited outside charity organizations called bread lines for hours, hoping to receive free food.

THE GREAT DEPRESSION

The Great Depression was a worldwide economic crisis. Shops closed, banks closed, and factories closed. In 1933, around 25 percent of American workers did not have a job. That's one out of every four people. Because so many people were unemployed, no one had money for things, even food. Prices of goods dropped. Farmers who had been able to grow things could not sell their crops. There was no one to buy them.

The dust storms started in 1932. Blowing wind swept the dry soil across the plains in dark clouds. There were only a few storms that year. People called them dusters.

The drought continued the next year. The dusters happened more often, and they grew stronger. A duster in November hit South Dakota like a blizzard. **Dunes** of dust covered fields and blocked roads.

The Dust Bowl has also been called the Dirty Thirties.

Dust and sand covered farm buildings and houses.

In 1934, the drought and dust were even worse. On the morning of May 9, 1934, a dust storm started in Wyoming, North Dakota, and South Dakota. The next day, 12 million pounds (5.4 million kilograms) of dust blew into and fell on Chicago—4 pounds (1.8 kg) of dust for every person in the city. Days later, dust covered streets in Boston, New York, and Washington, D.C. Even ships in the Atlantic Ocean that were 300 miles (483 kilometers) off the East Coast had dust on their decks. But the worst of all was yet to come.

CHAPTER 3

BLACK SUNDAY

The winter months of 1935 were dry and warm. In March, there was a duster nearly every day. Schools and offices closed in many towns. In Kansas, a 7-year-old boy got lost while trying to walk home. He was found dead in a drift of sand.

APPROACHING DUST STORM IN MIDDLE WEST

During some periods, the dust storms were so dark and strong that there was no visibility at all.

When the skies were clear on the morning of April 14, people were eager to go outside. They opened the windows and hung out the laundry. They didn't know a storm was coming.

Cold air blew down from Canada. It met warm air over the Dakotas. Usually, when cold air hits warm air, it makes a wall of thunderstorms with high winds and rain. But because of the drought, there was no moisture in the air. There was wind, but no rain. The wind picked up the dust.

People heard flocks of birds overhead. The birds were flying away from the dark clouds rushing into the Great Plains. As the storm approached, it looked like a black wall as tall as a mountain range.

Texans were used to dusters. But nothing could prepare them for what was coming.

The storm came so quickly that people barely had time to get in their houses. In the middle of the day, the sunny sky turned as dark as midnight. A girl in Oklahoma named Marg Scruggs went with her family into their cellar. "It was terrible," she remembered. "It was just black, the blackest I've ever seen."

People slammed the windows shut before the storm hit. But even with the windows closed, the strong winds blew dust into houses. People sat inside and coughed in the dusty air.

A farmer and teacher named Caroline Henderson wrote about the dust in her house in Texas. "Dust to breathe and dust to drink. Dust in the beds and in the flour bin, on dishes and walls and windows, in hair and eyes and ears and throats."

The dust cloud that blew across the plains reached 500 to 600 feet (152 to 183 km) high.

A girl in Texas named Trixie Brown went with her family to have a picnic that morning. When the storm hit, they ran to their car. Caught in the wind and dust, her father couldn't see to drive. They were trapped for hours.

When they arrived home, they found the windows had been left open. "We couldn't get in the house," she remembered. Rooms were filled with dust.

Many people had gone outside to enjoy the nice, sunny day. They were caught outside when the storm hit.

People took shelter in basements, tornado shelters, stores, fire stations, and anywhere else that got them out of the storm.

Many other people were stranded in cars on Black Sunday. A reporter named Robert Geiger was trapped in his car for two hours in Oklahoma. When he got back to town, he wrote a newspaper article about the storm.

Geiger wrote, "Residents of the southwestern dust bowl marked up another black duster today." He introduced the term that now describes the drought of the 1930s and the area where it hit hardest: the Dust Bowl.

Scientists estimate that 300 million tons of dirt were swept away by the Black Sunday storm. But the storm caused more damage than soil loss. In the weeks after, people across the plains went to the hospital with health problems. Some people even died.

The drought and dust storms continued after Black Sunday. For the rest of the 1930s, rainfall was below normal. Western Kansas suffered through a number of years with more than 100 days of dust storms.

Visibility was so poor that people could see only 60 to 300 feet (18 to 91 meters) in front of them.

After Black Sunday, people bought or made dust masks to protect their lungs. Others wore goggles to cover their eyes.

FACT
The blowing dust made breathing painful. It caused **pneumonia**, filling lungs with infection. Other people got strep throat or eye infections from **bacteria** in the dust.

The Great Plains became a desert. There was little to no rain. No crops grew. Many people decided they could no longer live there.

CHAPTER 4

HOW THE DUST BOWL CHANGED THE WEST

With their failed crops covered in dust, many farmers on the Plains had no money. Shop owners had no one to buy their goods. The drought forced hundreds of millions of people to leave the plains. Towns and country homes stood empty.

Mothers, fathers, and children drove west in packed cars and trucks. Some went to California. Many of those **migrants** came from Oklahoma. They were called Okies.

In the 1930s, California was still growing. The migrants gave California's population a boost. Many Okies settled in central California. They found work on farms there, picking fruit, vegetables, and cotton. Others found work in the fast-growing city of Los Angeles.

MIGRANT MOTHER

The photographs of Dorothea Lange showed people across the country how hard life was for migrants fleeing the Dust Bowl. Lange traveled across the western United States, taking photographs of poor families and unemployed workers. Her most famous photo, "Migrant Mother," shows a woman who was in a camp of migrants wanting to find work in California.

Lange usually kept records about people she photographed, but in this case, there are no known notes. Decades later, Florence Owens Thompson revealed she was the woman in the photo. A Cherokee woman originally from Oklahoma, Thompson raised her family in California.

For farmers who stayed on the Plains, the Dust Bowl changed how they raised crops. Less than two weeks after Black Sunday, Congress passed a law to protect the nation's soil.

The Soil **Conservation** Service, an office of the U.S. government, worked with farmers to improve how they used the land. Farmers plowed their fields differently to prevent **erosion**. They agreed not to plant crops on some parts of their land. This allowed the soil to restore its nutrients.

Hugh Hammond Bennett (right) worked to combat erosion after the Dust Bowl.

By 1938, trees were planted and land was re-plowed. The blowing soil was reduced by 65 percent. The next year, the rain returned.

Because of better soil conservation, the Great Plains are now a productive farming area. Today, wheat and corn from Kansas, Oklahoma, and Nebraska feed people across America and around the world. But there are fears that farmers are drawing too much water from deep wells. We all depend on crops from the Plains. Thanks to technology, scientists can closely monitor weather and land conditions. Hopefully, we will remember the lessons of the Dust Bowl.

TIMELINE

1862: The Homestead Act is signed into law by President Abraham Lincoln.

1909: The enlarged Homestead Act doubles the size of the land available for homesteaders.

1914: World War I begins. The cost of wheat and other crops goes up. The war ends in 1918.

1924: Rainfall on the Great Plains is far above normal levels.

1929: The Great Depression begins. It lasts for 10 years.

1931: Rainfall sinks below normal levels, starting the long period of drought.

MAY 10, 1934: A dust storm drops 12 million pounds (5.4 million kg) of dust on Chicago.

FEBRUARY–MARCH 1935: Dust storms hit the Great Plains nearly every day.

APRIL 14, 1935: The Black Sunday dust storm hits the Great Plains.

APRIL 27, 1935: Congress passes the Soil Conservation Act. It establishes the Soil Conservation Service.

1938: Millions of people leave the Great Plains. By 1940, 2.5 million people have left the area.

GLOSSARY

bacteria (bak-TEER-ee-uh)—one-celled, tiny living things; some are helpful and some cause disease

conservation (kon-ser-VAY-shuhn)—the wise use of natural resources to protect them from loss or being used up

drought (DROUT)—a long period of weather with little or no rainfall

dune (DOON)—a hill or ridge of sand piled up by the wind

erosion (ih-ROH-zhuhn)—the wearing away of land by water or wind

homestead (HOHM-sted)—a piece of land with room for a new home and farm

immigrant (IM-uh-gruhnt)—someone who comes from one country or place to live permanently in another country or place

irrigate (IHR-uh-gate)—to supply water for crops using channels or pipes

migrant (MY-gruhnt)—a person who moves to a new area or country, generally in search of work

nutrient (NOO-tree-uhnt)—a substance needed by a living thing to stay healthy

pneumonia (noo-MOH-nyuh)—a serious disease that causes the lungs to become inflamed and filled with a thick fluid that makes breathing difficult

READ MORE

Loh-Hagen, Virginia. *Famine and Dust: Dust Bowl.* Ann Arbor, MI: 45th Parallel Press, an imprint of Cherry Lake Publishing, 2019.

Roesser, Marie. *The Dust Bowl.* New York: Gareth Stevens Publishing, 2020.

Smith, Elliott. *Focus on the Great Depression.* Minneapolis: Lerner Publications, 2022.

INTERNET SITES

American History for Kids: The Dust Bowl
americanhistoryforkids.com/the-dust-bowl/

Britannica Kids: The Dust Bowl
kids.britannica.com/kids/article/Dust-Bowl/390020

The Dust Bowl for Kids
greatdepression.mrdonn.org/dustbowl.html

INDEX

Author Biography

Bruce Berglund was a history professor for 19 years. He taught courses on ancient and modern history, war and society, women's history, and sports history. Bruce was a Fulbright Scholar three times, and he has traveled to 16 different countries in Europe and Asia for research and teaching.